DINOSAURS

TYRANNOSAURUS REX

BY HEATHER C. HUDAK

An Imprint of Abdo Publishing
abdobooks.com

abdobooks.com

Published by Abdo Publishing, a division of ABDO, PO Box 398166, Minneapolis, Minnesota 55439.

Printed in the United States of America, North Mankato, Minnesota.
102023
012024

THIS BOOK CONTAINS RECYCLED MATERIALS

Cover Photo: iStockphoto
Interior Photos: Shutterstock Images, 4–5, 8, 14 (dinosaurs), 17; Claus Lunau/Science Source, 7; Paul D. Stewart/NaturePL/Science Source, 10; Herschel Hoffmeyer/Shutterstock Images, 12–13, 28–29; Eva Speshneva/Shutterstock Images, 14 (horse); Mario Tama/Getty Images News/Getty Images, 18; Marten Van Dijl/AFP/Getty Images, 20–21; Bettmann/Getty Images, 22; Genna Martin/San Francisco Chronicle/Hearst Newspapers/Getty Images, 24; Murray Close/Moviepix/Getty Images, 26

Editor: Marley Richmond
Series Designer: Mary Shaw

Library of Congress Control Number: 2023939656

Publisher's Cataloging-in-Publication Data

Names: Hudak, Heather C., author.
Title: Tyrannosaurus Rex / by Heather C. Hudak
Description: Minneapolis, Minnesota: Abdo Publishing, 2024 | Series: Dinosaurs | Includes online resources and index.
Identifiers: ISBN 9781098292713 (lib. bdg.) | ISBN 9798384910657 (ebook)
Subjects: LCSH: Dinosaurs--Juvenile literature. | Prehistoric animals--Juvenile literature. | Tyrannosaurus Rex--Juvenile literature.
Classification: DDC 567.90--dc23

CONTENTS

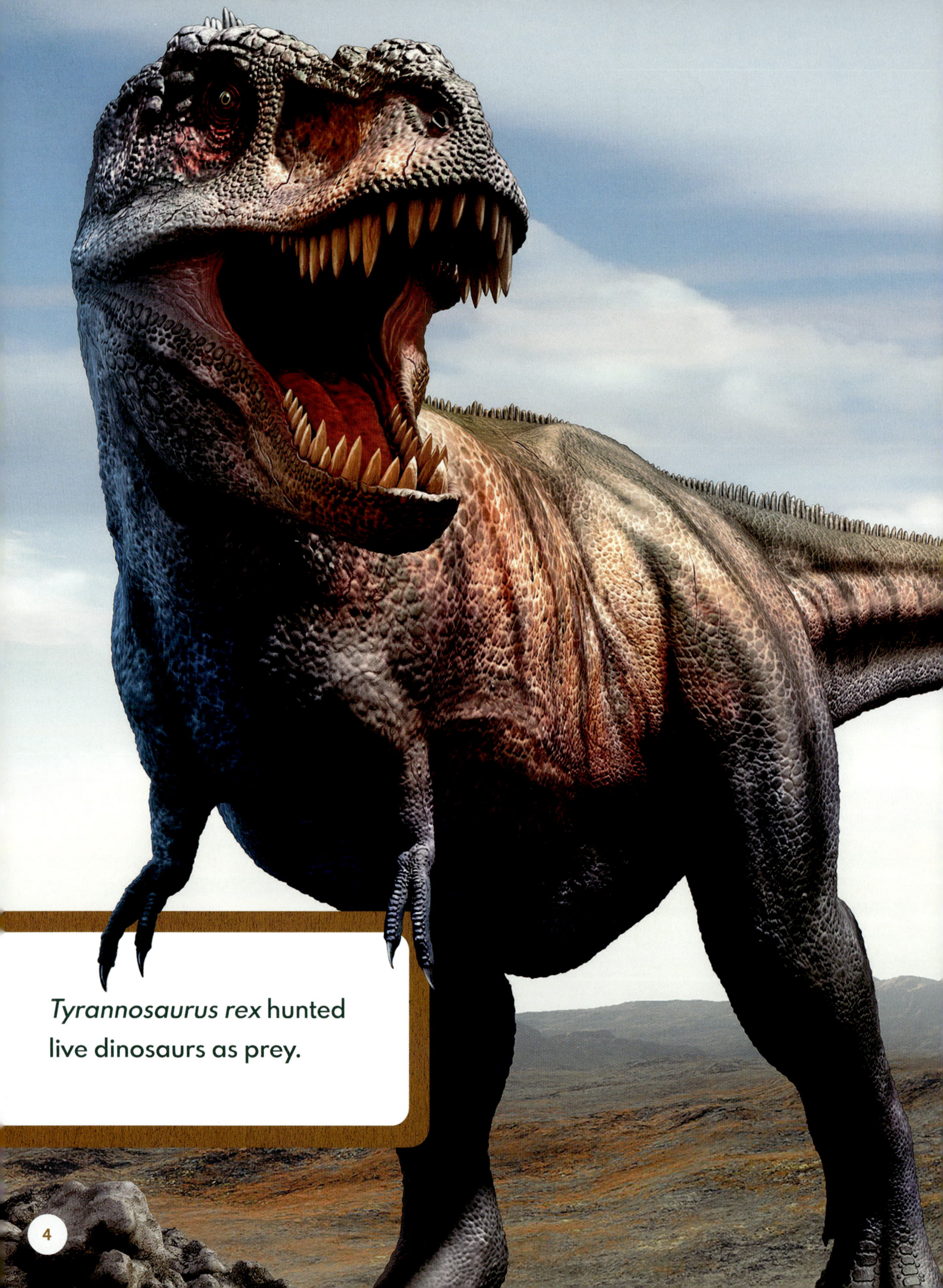

Tyrannosaurus rex hunted live dinosaurs as prey.

CHAPTER 1

BIG BEAST

It's hot in the midday sun. A *Triceratops* grazes on some flowering plants. Nearby, a herd of *Edmontosaurus* drinks from a river. Suddenly, the leaves rustle. The ground shakes. Something big is moving slowly through the trees. A fierce beast appears.

The dinosaur is huge. It is a *Tyrannosaurus rex* (teye-RAN-uh-SOHR-uhs reks), and it is hungry.

The herd of *Edmontosaurus* starts to run. They are faster than the *Tyrannosaurus rex (T. rex)*, but one of them stumbles. It is injured. It can't run away. The *T. rex* closes in. It is about to grab the *Edmontosaurus* in its jaws. Then, a second *T. rex* appears. It moves toward the injured *Edmontosaurus.* At the last second, it changes course. It attacks the other *T. rex* instead. The two giant dinosaurs bite at each other's faces. They are fighting over the prey.

The two *T. rex* battle fiercely. After the fight, the winning *T. rex* turns to the injured *Edmontosaurus.* It eats its prey.

Scientists have found *T. rex* skulls with gashes on them. These scars are evidence that *T. rex* fought one another.

Alligators are modern-day reptiles. They have jaws that are similar to those of *T. rex*.

Prehistoric Period

T. rex is just one of about 700 known dinosaur species. Dinosaurs were **prehistoric** reptiles. They first appeared about 245 million years ago. They ranged in size from 8 pounds (3.6 kg) to 160,000 pounds (72,600 kg). The smallest dinosaur would have weighed about as much as a cat. The heaviest dinosaur could have weighed as much as seven African elephants, which are the biggest land animals in the world today.

Long, Long Ago

T. rex roamed Earth during the Late Cretaceous period. The Cretaceous period was about 145 million to 66 million years ago. *T. rex* lived between 90 million and 66 million years ago. Billions of *T. rex* might have lived and died during this time.

Scientists saw a connection between dinosaurs and birds when they discovered *Archaeopteryx*. It was a dinosaur with feathery wings.

Dinosaurs went **extinct** about 66 million years ago. But some of their **descendants** are still around today. Dinosaurs were the ancestors of all modern bird species. In fact, chickens, ostriches, and alligators are all related to *T. rex*. *T. rex* is now one of the best-known dinosaurs.

Further Evidence

Look at the website below. Does it give any new evidence to support Chapter One?

Dinosaur Facts

abdocorelibrary.com/tyrannosaurus-rex

Young *T. rex* grew quickly. They could gain up to 6 pounds (2.7 kg) every day.

CHAPTER 2

APEX PREDATOR

Tyrannosaurus rex was one of the largest meat-eating dinosaurs. Its name means "king of the tyrant lizards" in Latin. As an adult, it stood up to 12 feet (3.6 m) tall. It was more than 40 feet (12 m) long. *T. rex* could weigh as much as 15,500 pounds (7,030 kg).

Giant Dinosaurs

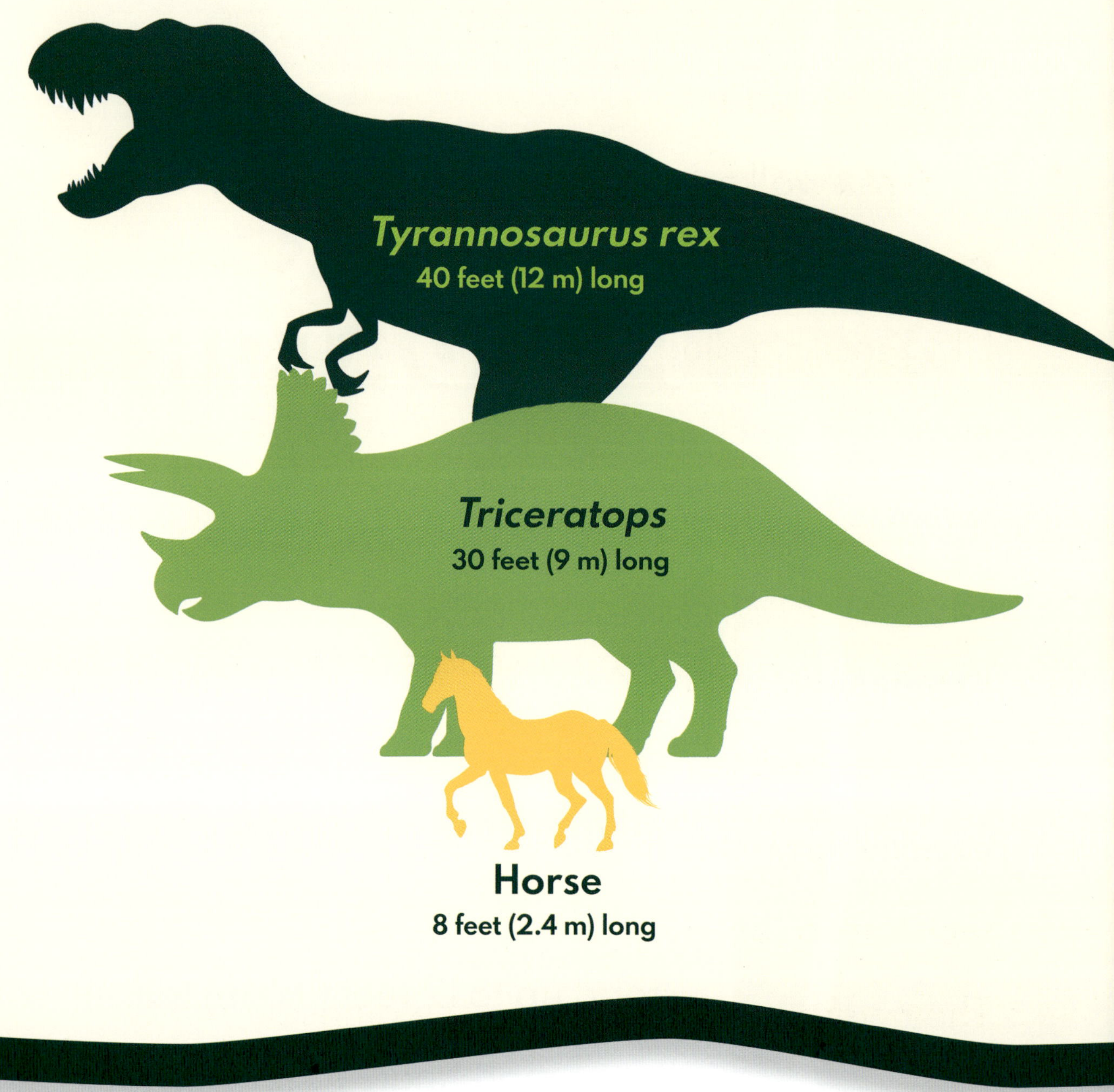

T. rex was one of the largest meat-eating dinosaurs during the Cretaceous period. It hunted dinosaurs such as *Triceratops*, which were close to its own size! *T. rex* would have been five times the length of an average horse today.

That is about the same size as an average African elephant.

T. rex walked on two legs. It had strong thighs. Its big tail balanced out its heavy head. Like most big dinosaurs, *T. rex* probably did not move quickly. The dinosaur was too big to run fast. It walked at about 3 miles per hour (4.8 km/h). It may have run at speeds up to 15 miles per hour (24 km/h).

T. rex had very short arms. No one knows exactly why its arms were so short or what they were used for. They were just 3 feet (0.9 m) long. They were too short to help the dinosaur hunt or eat.

T. rex had a huge head. It was up to 5 feet (1.5 m) long and held up by a thick neck.

T. rex had a strong sense of smell, which it used to find food.

Meat Eater

T. rex was a carnivore. It ate meat. It was an apex predator, which means it was at the top of the food chain. Other dinosaurs likely feared it. *T. rex* mainly preyed on large herbivores, such as *Triceratops* and *Edmontosaurus*.

Bare Bones

Dinosaur bones formed rings as they aged. Scientists use the rings to tell how old a dinosaur was and how quickly it reached its full size. *T. rex* were fully grown by about 20 years of age. The oldest-known *T. rex* was about 28 years old when it died.

T. rex had eyes that were in the front of its head. Their position helped *T. rex* tell how far away it was from its prey.

T. rex had large teeth and the strongest bite of any land animal in history.

Its powerful jaws had about 60 **serrated** teeth. Each tooth could be up to 8 inches (20 cm) long. *T. rex* had a bone-crushing bite. Its jaws were so strong they could have crushed a car. But *T. rex* probably did not chew its food. After tearing into its prey, *T. rex* gulped its meals down in chunks. It even ate the bones.

PRIMARY SOURCE

David Burnham is a **paleontologist**. He said *T. rex* was so huge that it was hard for the dinosaur to find enough food.

> *T. rex* . . . may have fed on carcasses, but that is not a very **abundant** or consistent food source. *T. rex* had a hard life. They had to go out and kill for food when they were hungry.

Source: Joseph Castro. "*Tyrannosaurus Rex:* King of the Dinosaurs." *Live Science*, 17 Oct. 2017, livescience.com. Accessed 8 Mar. 2023.

Comparing Texts

Think about the quote. Does it support the information in this chapter? Or does it give a different perspective? Explain how in a few sentences.

Scientists have discovered fossils from fewer than 100 individual *T. rex*.

DIG DEEP

T. rex lived in what is now North America. *T. rex* fossils have been found in a few parts of the United States and Canada, including Montana, Utah, New Mexico, South Dakota, Alberta, and Saskatchewan.

Barnum Brown found the first *T. rex* fossils. He was a **paleontologist**. Brown found the first partial *T. rex* skeleton in Hell Creek, Montana, in 1902. Six years later, Brown and his team found a more complete *T. rex* skeleton. This *T. rex* is on display at the American Museum of Natural History in New York City.

Barnum Brown and his workers laid out the *T. rex* fossils they found.

Sue and Scotty

In August 1990, paleontologist Sue Hendrickson was searching for fossils on a South Dakota ranch. There, Hendrickson discovered one of the biggest *T. rex* skeletons. The *T. rex* was nicknamed Sue after her. About 90 percent of the *T. rex's* bones were found. Sue the *T. rex* is on display at the Field Museum in Chicago, Illinois.

About one year after Sue was found, there was another major *T. rex* discovery. A high school teacher named Robert Gebhardt found a tooth and a tailbone in Saskatchewan, Canada. After some digging, researchers found more parts of a *T. rex* skeleton. They nicknamed this *T. rex* Scotty. Scotty can be seen at the Royal Saskatchewan Museum in Canada.

Scientists must be very careful with fossils. Bones must be cleaned and prepared so they do not break down.

Scientists think that Scotty weighed nearly 20,000 pounds (9,070 kg) when the *T. rex* was alive. Scotty is the heaviest *T. rex* on record.

Movie Mania

T. rex has been featured in many movies and books. It played a major role in the *Jurassic Park* movies. But not everything about *T. rex* in *Jurassic Park* is accurate.

In the movies, *T. rex* runs much faster than it did in real life. Its roar sounds like a lion. No one knows for sure what *T. rex* sounded like.

Dinosaur Dating

To learn how long ago *T. rex* lived, scientists measure the amount of certain elements in rocks around dinosaur fossils. These elements **decay** at a steady rate over time. Scientists can tell how old the rock is by how much of the element has decayed.

The *T. rex* in *Jurassic Park* has terrible eyesight. But this was not true about the dinosaur in real life.

But it likely sounded more like a bird or crocodile. *T. rex* was probably covered in scales, like it is in the movie. But scientists think it also may have had some feathers.

There are still many mysteries about *T. rex*. But paleontologists continue to learn more about these massive predators. Every fossil discovery gives them information about the past. These clues help them piece together the prehistoric story of *T. rex*.

Explore Online

Visit the website below. Does it give any new information about *T. rex* fossils that wasn't in Chapter Three?

Ask a Scientist about *T. rex*

abdocorelibrary.com/tyrannosaurus-rex

DINO DETAILS

Thick neck to hold up its massive head

Sharp, sawlike teeth to tear into its meals

Strong jaws to crush bones

Heavy tail to help balance the weight of its head

Glossary

abundant
having lots of something

decay
to break down over time due to natural forces

descendants
relatives that come from something that lived in the past

extinct
no longer exists

paleontologist
a scientist who studies fossils

prehistoric
having to do with the time before written history

serrated
jagged or notched

Online Resources

To learn more about *Tyrannosaurus rex*, visit our free resource websites below.

Visit **abdocorelibrary.com** or scan this QR code for free Common Core resources for teachers and students, including vetted activities, multimedia, and booklinks, for deeper subject comprehension.

Visit **abdobooklinks.com** or scan this QR code for free additional online weblinks for further learning. These links are routinely monitored and updated to provide the most current information available.

Learn More

Hulick, Kathryn. *Dinosaurs.* Abdo, 2023.

Lambert, David. *Dinosaur.* DK, 2021.

Vallepur, Shalini. *Dino Trek for a Tyrannosaurus Rex.* BookLife, 2023.

Index

About the Author

Heather C. Hudak has written hundreds of kids' books on all kinds of topics. When she is not writing, Heather loves to travel. She has spent several weekends looking for dinosaur fossils near the Royal Tyrrell Museum in the badlands of Alberta.